DISCOVERING THE UNITED STATES

Colorado

BY HALEY WILLIAMS

Kids Core

An Imprint of Abdo Publishing
abdobooks.com

abdobooks.com

Printed in China.
052024
092024

Cover Photo: John Morrison/iStockphoto
Interior Photos: Jim West/imageBROKER/GmbH & Co. KG/Alamy, 4–5; Filip Bjorkman/Shutterstock Images, 6; David Spates/Shutterstock Images, 9 (top left); Shutterstock Images, 9 (top right), 18, 20–21, 26; Hale Kell/Shutterstock Images, 9 (bottom left); Paul Barron/Shutterstock Images, 9 (bottom right); Tassanee Riebpadith/Shutterstock Images, 10; Ian Dagnall/Alamy, 12–13; Crystal Ashike/Global Press/Alamy, 14; Brent Hofacker/Shutterstock Images, 16; Jacob Boomsma/Shutterstock Images, 22, 28 (Colorado Springs); T. Schofield/Shutterstock Images, 23; Tom Tietz/Shutterstock Images, 25; Red Line Editorial, 28 (map), 29; John Hoffman/Shutterstock Images, 28 (Pikes Peak); Eric Brinley/Shutterstock Images, 28 (sand dunes)

Editor: Marley Richmond
Series Designer: Katharine Hale

Library of Congress Control Number: 2023949355

Publisher's Cataloging-in-Publication Data

Names: Williams, Haley, author.
Title: Colorado / by Haley Williams
Description: Minneapolis, Minnesota: Abdo Publishing, 2025 | Series: Discovering the United States | Includes online resources and index.
Identifiers: ISBN 9781098293765 (lib. bdg.) | ISBN 9798384913030 (ebook)
Subjects: LCSH: U.S. states--Juvenile literature. | Colorado--History--Juvenile literature. | Western States (U.S.)--Juvenile literature. | Physical geography--United States--Juvenile literature.
Classification: DDC 973--dc23

All population data taken from:
"Estimates of Population by Sex, Race, and Hispanic Origin: April 1, 2020 to July 1, 2022." *US Census Bureau, Population Division*, June 2023, census.gov.

CONTENTS

Scientists have found dinosaur footprints in Morrison, Colorado.

CHAPTER 1

Digging for Dinosaurs

It was March 20, 1877. A professor named Arthur Lakes was walking on a hill in Morrison, Colorado. He and a small group were searching for **fossils**. Lakes noticed a large bone in the ground. It looked like it might be a bone from a dinosaur.

Colorado's flag represents nature in the state. The gold circle is a symbol for sunshine. White represents the snowy mountains. Blue represents the sky. Red is for Colorado's soil.

Lakes wasn't sure what dinosaur the bone came from. He wondered if there could be more fossils there.

That day, Lakes discovered the first *Stegosaurus* fossil ever found. He was also the first person to find fossils from several other dinosaurs. Scientists used these fossils to learn more about dinosaurs that lived in Colorado millions of years ago. The area is now known as Dinosaur Ridge. People can visit and learn all about the dinosaurs that lived there.

Colorado's Land

Colorado is located in the US region called the West. It borders six other states. Wyoming is to the north, and Nebraska is to the north and east. Kansas is also to the east. Oklahoma and New Mexico are to the south. Utah is to the west.

Colorado's land is different throughout the state. There are forests, mountains, canyons, and deserts. Eastern Colorado is covered in grasslands. This area is known as the Eastern Plains. Western Colorado has many mountain ranges. The tallest mountain is Mount Elbert. It stands 14,433 feet (4,399 m) tall.

The state is well-known for its wildlife. Larger animals found there include elk, mountain lions,

A State by Many Names

Colorado is known as the Centennial State. It got this nickname because it became a state 100 years after the Declaration of Independence was signed. Colorful Colorado is another popular nickname. It comes from the beautiful scenery throughout the state.

Colorado Facts

DATE OF STATEHOOD
August 1, 1876

CAPITAL
Denver

POPULATION
5,839,926

AREA
104,094 square miles
(269,602 sq km)

STATE BIRD

Lark bunting

STATE TREE

Colorado blue spruce

STATE FLOWER

Columbine

STATE FOSSIL

Stegosaurus

Each US state has a different population, size, and capital city. States also have state symbols.

moose, bighorn sheep, black bears, and bison. Smaller animals such as prairie dogs and rattlesnakes also live in Colorado.

Places with high elevation are colder than places with low elevation. Some mountains in Colorado are so tall that they have snowy peaks all year.

The Climate in Colorado

Colorado's climate varies throughout the state. This is partly because of changes in **elevation**.

In general, the climate in Colorado is cool and dry. The state has four seasons.

In the summer, some areas of Colorado can be 95 degrees Fahrenheit (35°C) or hotter. It rains a lot in the summer. This may cause flooding. Winters usually bring a lot of snow. In the mountains, snow often falls from November to mid-May. Other areas may experience snowfall as early as September.

Further Evidence

Look at the website below. Does it give any new evidence to support Chapter One?

Colorado

abdocorelibrary.com/discovering-colorado

In Mesa Verde National Park, visitors can see buildings made and used by Pueblo people in the early 1200s.

The People of Colorado

American Indian peoples have lived in Colorado for thousands of years. They include the Apache, Arapaho, Cheyenne, Pueblo, Shoshone, and Ute. The Southern Utes and Ute Mountain Utes are the only federally recognized tribes in Colorado.

Many American Indian people wear traditional clothes to take part in the Southern Ute Bear Dance celebration.

The Utes are one of the oldest American Indian peoples in the state. They **migrated** to southwestern Colorado in about 1300 CE. The Utes were **nomads**. Nature is an important part of Ute culture. Spring is celebrated with a dance called the bear dance. This dance is still an important part of Ute culture.

White **settlers** came to Colorado in the mid-1700s and early 1800s. They were mostly from France and Spain. But people from Mexico also settled in the state. Today, about 67 percent of Coloradans are white. Hispanic or Latino people make up 23 percent of the population. About 5 percent of people are Black, and 2 percent are American Indian. In 2022, about 5.8 million people lived in Colorado.

Many people eat *chile verde* as a soup. But it is also served with beans and rice or on top of burritos.

Culture and Jobs in Colorado

Many foods in Colorado come from Spanish, Mexican, and American Indian peoples. A popular dish in the state is green chili, or *chile verde*. It is a spicy stew that usually includes pork and green chilis. Sweet corn is also a popular food in Colorado.

Sports are a big part of Colorado culture. Denver is one of ten cities in the United States with five professional sports teams. Many Coloradans like to cheer for the Denver Broncos football team.

Colorado has a few major industries. The biggest industry is **manufacturing**. Aerospace manufacturing is important there.

Winter Fun

Skiing and snowboarding are big parts of Colorado culture. Millions of people from around the United States and other countries visit the many ski resorts in Colorado every year. A few of the most popular ski towns include Vail, Breckenridge, Telluride, and Aspen.

More than 10,000 people work at ski resorts in Colorado every year. Some of these people teach skiing lessons.

This includes the design and creation of planes, helicopters, and space vehicles. Tourism is another top industry. Jobs in this industry include those at ski resorts. Other tourism jobs are in transportation or food services.

Primary Source

Bear dance chief Matthew J. Box has helped organize the bear dance for many years. He discusses the importance of the dance for the Ute people today and throughout history:

> The dance enhances a bigger picture for our people. . . . It provides in many ways for the Utes, especially healing, and that's why it's still here.

Source: Damon Toledo. "History of the Bear Dance." *Southern Ute Drum*, 17 Apr. 2015, sudrum.com. Accessed 22 Aug. 2023.

What's the Big Idea?

Read this quote carefully. What is its main idea? Explain how the main idea is supported by details.

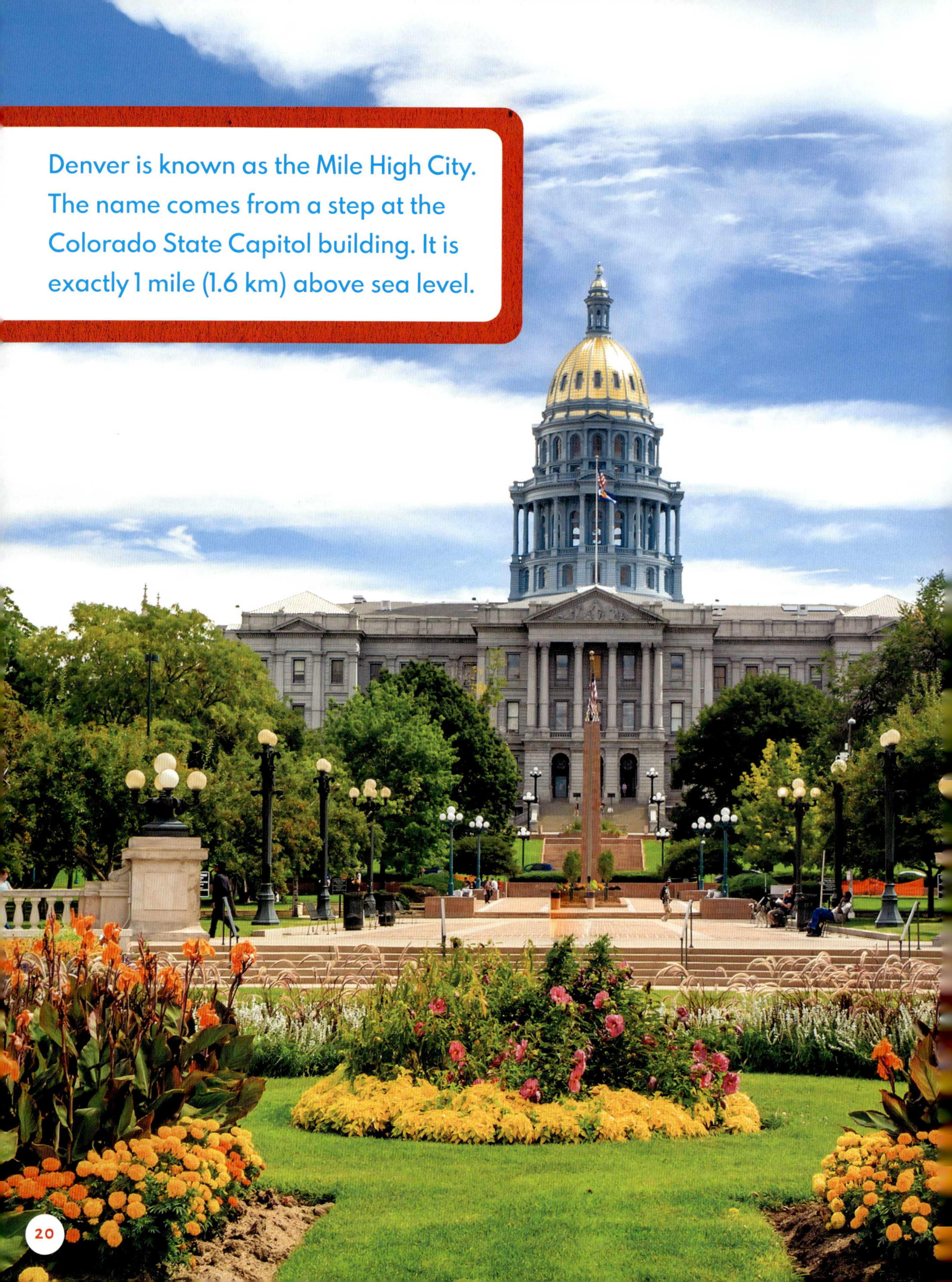

Denver is known as the Mile High City. The name comes from a step at the Colorado State Capitol building. It is exactly 1 mile (1.6 km) above sea level.

CHAPTER 3

Places in Colorado

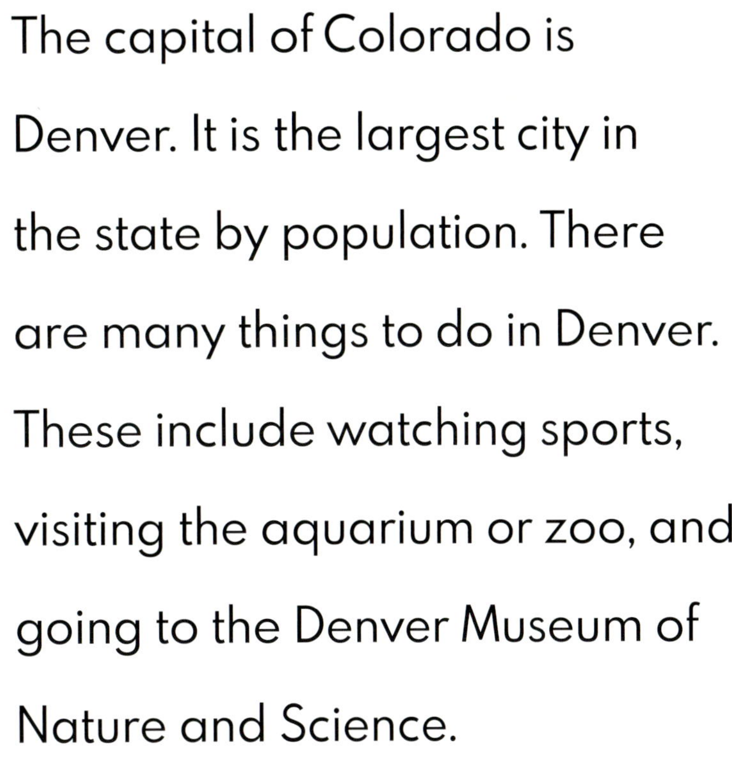

The capital of Colorado is Denver. It is the largest city in the state by population. There are many things to do in Denver. These include watching sports, visiting the aquarium or zoo, and going to the Denver Museum of Nature and Science.

Colorado Springs is named after the Manitou Springs. These eight freshwater springs are to the west of the city. Their water comes from snow melting off Pikes Peak.

Colorado Springs is the second-largest city in Colorado by population. The mountain Pikes Peak is found there. It is the most well-known mountain in the state.

Black Canyon of the Gunnison National Park has steep cliffs. The canyon is 48 miles (77 km) long and up to 2,700 feet (820 m) deep.

National Parks

Colorado has four National Parks. They are Rocky Mountain, Great Sand Dunes, Mesa Verde, and Black Canyon of the Gunnison. The land of these parks is protected by the US government.

Rocky Mountain National Park is one of the most visited parks in the nation. The park covers about 415 square miles (1,075 sq km) of Colorado.

There are many kinds of environments in the park, including mountains, forests, and **alpine tundra**. It is known for its beautiful scenery and wildlife.

Great Sand Dunes National Park

Great Sand Dunes National Park has the highest sand dunes in North America. The tallest dune is about 750 feet (230 m) tall. Some people enjoy sledding down the mountains of sand or hiking up them.

Colorado's name comes from Spanish and means "colored red." Many rocks in the state are reddish, including those at the Colorado National Monument.

Landmarks

There are many human-made and natural landmarks in Colorado. The Colorado National Monument is in the western part of the state.

Lake Granby is in Rocky Mountain National Park. The lake connects to the Colorado River.

Large red rock formations can be found throughout the monument. Visitors can hike, camp, and bike there.

The Colorado River begins in Rocky Mountain National Park. It runs through seven states and is about 1,450 miles (2,330 km) long. Many people go fishing or boating on the Colorado River.

The Four Corners Monument is another important landmark. It is the only place in the United States where four states meet.

Those states are Colorado, Utah, New Mexico, and Arizona. There are also several historical American Indian sites near the monument.

Colorado has plenty of natural locations for visitors to explore. People can also try popular dishes in Denver or go skiing in the mountains. Colorado offers a variety of places to see and things to do.

Explore Online

Visit the website below. Does it give any new information about the Rocky Mountains that wasn't in Chapter Three?

Rocky Mountains

abdocorelibrary.com/discovering-colorado

State Map

Pikes Peak

KEY

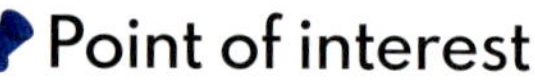

Capital | Park | City or town | Point of interest

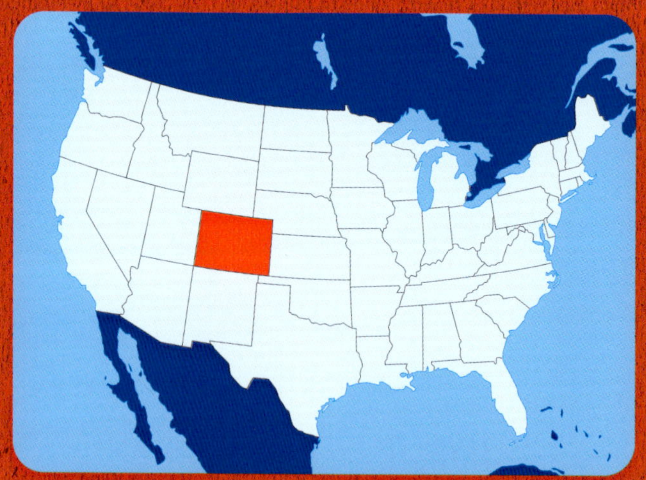

Great Sand Dunes National Park

Colorado Springs

Colorado: The Centennial State
Wyoming
Nebraska
Utah
Rocky Mountain National Park
Fort Collins
South Platte River
Boulder
Denver
Colorado River
Dinosaur Ridge
Colorado National Monument
Aspen
Pikes Peak
Colorado Springs
Black Canyon of the Gunnison National Park
Kansas
Arkansas River
Four Corners National Monument
Great Sand Dunes National Park and Preserve
N
W
E
S
Mesa Verde National Park
Arizona
New Mexico
Oklahoma

Glossary

alpine tundra
a cold, treeless environment located in the mountains

elevation
the height above sea level

fossil
the very old, preserved remains of an animal or plant

manufacturing
the process of making goods to sell

migrated
permanently moved from one place to another

nomads
people who don't live in one place but who move from place to place

settlers
people who moved to a new area

Online Resources

To learn more about Colorado, visit our free resource websites below.

Visit **abdocorelibrary.com** or scan this QR code for free Common Core resources for teachers and students, including vetted activities, multimedia, and booklinks, for deeper subject comprehension.

Visit **abdobooklinks.com** or scan this QR code for free additional online weblinks for further learning. These links are routinely monitored and updated to provide the most current information available.

Learn More

Earley, Christina. *Colorado*. Crabtree, 2023.

Troutman, Alex. *Critters of Colorado: Pocket Guide to Animals in Your State*. Adventure, 2024.

Index

About the Author

Haley Williams is an editor who lives in Minnesota. She lived in Colorado for almost 20 years. Her favorite thing to do when she lived in Colorado was to go hiking with her family in the bluffs near her home.